This Beautiful Land
IRELAND

This Beautiful Land
IRELAND

John Freeman and Sue Sharpe

Bison Books

Published by
Bison Books Ltd
176 Old Brompton Road
London SW5
England

ISBN 0-86124-248-3

Printed in Hong Kong

Page 1: *The High Cross of Moone, County Kildare.*
Pages 2–3: *The Sneem River runs alongside the Catholic church at Sneem, County Kerry.*
Below: *Dalkey Bay, south of Dublin, is reminiscent of the Mediterranean.*

Acknowledgments

The publishers would like to thank the
following individuals and agencies for their
help in the preparation of this book:

Aughnanure Castle
Bord Fáilte Irish Tourist Board
Bronica UK Ltd
ITGWU Dublin
The Irish National Stud
Northern Ireland Tourist Board
Powerscourt Estate
The Curragh Race Course
The Board of Trinity College, Dublin
Martin Bristow, the designer

Contents

Ulster

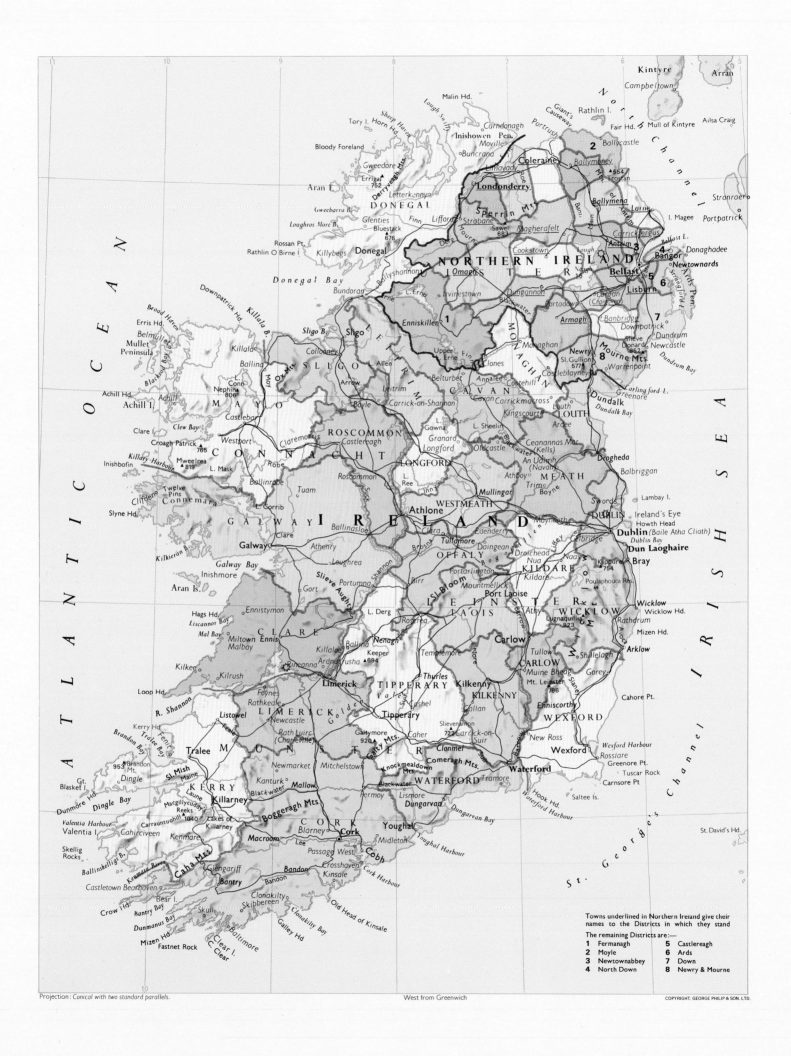

ATLANTIC OCEAN

Kintyre
Campbeltown
Arran
Ailsa Craig
Mull of Kintyre
Fair Hd.
Stranraer
Portpatrick
I. Magee

NORTH CHANNEL

Malin Hd.
Tory I.
Horn Hd.
Sheep Haven
Lough Swilly
Carndonagh
Inishowen Pen.
Moville
Buncrana
Giant's Causeway
Rathlin I.
Portrush
Ballycastle
Ballymoney
2
Bloody Foreland
Gweedore
Errigal 752
Derryveagh Mts.
Letterkenny
Coleraine
Limavady
Londonderry
Trostan ▲554
Ballymena
Larne
Aran I.
DONEGAL
Glenties
Bluestack 676
Finn
Lifford
Strabane
Sperrin Mts.
Sawel 683
Magherafelt
Antrim
Carrickfergus
Belfast L.
Rossan Pt.
Rathlin O Birne I.
Killybegs
Donegal
Cookstown
Lough Neagh 16
Belfast
Bangor
Donaghadee
Newtownards
Ards Pen.
Killala B.
Downpatrick Hd.
Killala
Ballyshannon
L. Erne
NORTHERN IRELAND ULSTER
1 Omagh
Irvinestown
Dungannon
Portadown
Lurgan (Craigavon)
Lisburn
5
6
Strangford L.
Erris Hd.
Belmullet
Mullet Peninsula
Bundoran
Lower L. Erne
Enniskillen
Upper Erne
Clones
Annalee
Cootehill
Monaghan
Blackwater
Armagh
Banbridge
Downpatrick
Slieve Donard 852
Dundrum
Newcastle
Dundrum Bay
7
Broad Haven
Achill Hd.
Achill
Achill I.
Blacksod Bay
Clare I.
Nephin 806
L. Conn
Ballina
Moy
Sligo B.
Sligo
Collooney
LEITRIM
L. Allen
Arrow
Boyle
Carrick-on-Shannon
Belturbet
CAVAN
Cavan
Carrickmacross
Kingscourt
Ceanannas Mor (Kells)
Newry
Sl. Gullion 577
8
Mourne Mts.
Warrenpoint
Carlingford L.
Greenore
Dundalk
Dundalk Bay
SLIGO
Castlebar
Westport
Croagh Patrick ▲ 765
Mweelrea ▲ 819
Clew Bay
MAYO
CONNACHT
Claremorris
Castlereagh
ROSCOMMON
Gowna
Granard
Longford
LONGFORD
Oldcastle
L. Sheelin
Ardee
LOUTH
Louth
Drogheda
Balbriggan
Inishbofin
Killary Harbour
Twelve Pins
Connemara
Slyne Hd.
L. Mask
Ballinrobe
Robe
Roscommon
Suck
L. Ree
Inny
Athboy
Trim
Boyne
MEATH
An Uaimh (Navan)
Clifden
Tuam
Mullingar
WESTMEATH
Swords
Lambay I.
L. Corrib
Athlone
Moynooth
DUBLIN
Ireland's Eye
Howth Head
GALWAY
IRELAND
Clara
Edenderry
Allen
Liffey
Dublin (Baile Átha Cliath)
Galway
Clare
Athenry
Loughrea
Ballinasloe
Brosna
OFFALY
Tullamore
Daingean
Drichead Nua
Celbridge
Naas
Clane
Dun Laoghaire
Dublin Bay
Aran Is.
Galway Bay
Inishmore
Slieve Aughty
Portumna
Shannon
Birr
Portarlington
Mountmellick
LSI. BLOOM
Kildare
KILDARE
Kippure ▲ 754
Poulaphouca Res.
Bray
Hags Hd.
Liscannor Bay
Ennistymon
L. Derg
Port Laoise
LAOIS
Athy
WICKLOW
Lugnaquillia 923
Wicklow
Wicklow Hd.
Mal Bay
Miltown Malbay
Ennis
CLARE
Killaloe
Ballina
Nenagh
Keeper ▲ 694
Roscrea
Mt. Leinster 796
Rathdrum
Mizen Hd.
Kilkee
Kilrush
Bunratty
Ardnacrusha
Templemore
Muine Bheag
Tullow
Shillelagh
Arklow
Loop Hd.
Foynes
Rathkeale
Limerick
TIPPERARY
Thurles
Cashel
KILKENNY
Carlow
Gorey
R. Shannon
Listowel
Newcastle
LIMERICK
Golden Vale
Tipperary
Kilkenny
Callan
CARLOW
Cahore Pt.
Kerry Hd.
Feale
Rath Luirc (Charleville)
Galtymore 920 ▲
Galty Mts.
Caher
Slievenamon 722
Carrick-on-Suir
New Ross
Enniscorthy
WEXFORD
Brandon Bay
Tralee Bay
Tralee
MUNSTER
Newmarket
Mitchelstown
Clonmel
Wexford
Wexford Harbour
Rosslare
Tuscar Rock
Carnsore Pt.
Brandon 953 Mt.
Dingle
Sl. Mish
Maine
KERRY
Kanturk
Blackwater
Mallow
Knockmealdown Mts.
Comeragh Mts.
Waterford
Tramore
Gt. Blasket I.
Dunmore Hd.
Dingle Bay
Laune
Killarney
Fermoy
Blackwater
WATERFORD
Lismore
Dungarvan
Dungarvan Bay
Hook Hd.
Waterford Harbour
Saltee Is.
St. David's Hd.
Valentia Harbour
Macgillycuddy's Reeks
Carrauntoohill 1040
Lakes of Killarney
Boggeragh Mts.
CORK
Youghal
Youghal Harbour
Valentia I.
Cahirciveen
Kenmare
Lee
Macroom
Blarney
Cork
Midleton
Skellig Rocks
Ballinskelligs B.
Kenmare River
Caha Mts.
Glengariff
Bantry
Passage West
Bandon
Cobh
Crosshaven
Kinsale
Cork Harbour
Castletown Bearhaven
Bear I.
Bantry Bay
Clonakilty
Skibbereen
Bandon
Old Head of Kinsale
Crow Hd.
Dunmanus Hd.
Skull
Clonakilty Bay
Mizen Hd.
Baltimore
Clear I.
C. Clear
Fastnet Rock
Galley Hd.

IRISH SEA

ST. GEORGE'S CHANNEL

Greenore Pt.

Towns underlined in Northern Ireland give their names to the Districts in which they stand

The remaining Districts are:—

1	Fermanagh	**5**	Castlereagh
2	Moyle	**6**	Ards
3	Newtownabbey	**7**	Down
4	North Down	**8**	Newry & Mourne

Projection: Conical with two standard parallels.

West from Greenwich

COPYRIGHT. GEORGE PHILIP & SON. LTD.

Ulster is the most northerly province in Ireland. It included nine counties until 1922 when six – Antrim, Armagh, Down, Fermanagh, Londonderry and Tyrone – were combined to form Northern Ireland and granted partial self-government under the British Crown. The remaining counties of Cavan, Monaghan and Donegal became part of the Irish Free State, now the Irish Republic.

Ulster has witnessed a stormy history which, like the rest of Ireland, has been a chronicle of foreign invasion and struggle for land ownership and religious freedom. Unlike the Irish Republic, the situation of Northern Ireland has yet to be resolved.

The northern Ulster coast looks over a narrow strip of sea to Scotland, and the landscapes of the two countries reveal many similarities. The Ulster hills were a continuation of the Scottish highlands and uplands, and the Sperrin Mountains in north Tyrone turn purple-brown with heather in late summer. These contrast with brown boglands in

Previous pages: *Glenelly Valley, at the foot of the Sperrin Mountains, County Tyrone.*
Left: *A map of Ireland.*
Below: *Ballyness Bay, County Donegal.*

the west, and green central lowlands punctuated by lakes and rivers. The province is bounded by sea on three sides, resulting in a profusion of rocky headlands, rugged cliffs, tidal inlets and sandy beaches.

The vast expanse of Lough Neagh, where five of Northern Ireland's six counties meet, is the collapsed central area of a mass of volcanic lava. The same volcanic rocks are associated with the Inner Hebrides, the Faroes and Iceland. Some of the region's most distinctive landmarks are formed from this lava – Antrim's terraced sea cliffs, Cavehill, overlooking Belfast, and the Giant's Causeway.

Ireland's history goes back a long way; the earliest Celts, who made a great impact on the country, may have arrived from central Europe in the 6th Century BC. But its history is often dated from the introduction of Christianity in the 5th Century, associated with the arrival of St Patrick, the patron saint of Ireland. From the 9th Century the country was invaded several times over, first by the Vikings, and later by the Normans in the 12th Century.

The Anglo-Normans made little headway in the north of Ireland compared with central and southern areas. It was not until the 16th Century that this area became a focal point,

when Elizabeth I, fearing a Spanish attack through Ireland, launched several military expeditions against Ulster. These were vigorously repelled by the Earl of Tyrone and the Lord of Tyrconnel, but they were defeated in 1601 and had to flee the country.

Catholic Ireland was now dominated by the superior force of Protestant England. Religious differences became the cornerstone of national animosity. Irish Catholic resentment created insecurity in the English, who saw the best solution in uprooting the hostile native population and replacing them with loyal Protestants. The so-called 'Flight of the Irish Earls' paved the way for this 'plantation'. James I of England confiscated their lands and installed thousands of Scottish and English settlers. Increasing attempts were made to suppress Catholicism and spread Anglicanism. The Gaelic Irish of Ulster rebelled in 1641; they were ruthlessly crushed by Cromwell in 1649 after the end of the Civil War in England.

Ulster was rapidly becoming a province with two populations, one of Gaelic-speaking Catholics and the other of English-speaking Protestants. In Ulster today, Irish as a spoken language has almost vanished except in the north and west of Killybegs, County Donegal.

In Glencolumbkill, on the Slieve League peninsula, courses are held in Irish language and culture, and Ireland's past is relived through the Folk Museum, which contains exact replicas of local dwelling houses between 1700 and 1900. In the mist and rain so common to this coast, these cottages, with their roped-down thatch and primitive contents, effectively portray the struggle to exist of ordinary folk during this period.

Close to Donegal lies the city of Derry, granted to the City of London Corporation in 1610 as part of the extensive Londonderry plantation. In 1688 William of Orange seized the English throne from Catholic James II, who fled to France. The next year James landed in Ulster where Derry's city governor was willing to accommodate his troops, but a group of apprentices closed the gates. This was the start of the Siege of Londonderry, when 30,000 people were besieged by Royalists for 105 days. Many died of disease and starvation before the city was relieved by three merchant ships that broke through the Jacobite barrier across the River Foyle. The following year, 1690, William defeated James at the famous Battle of the Boyne, which sealed the Protestant victory and left Irish Catholics politically helpless. Two years later Catholics were excluded from the Irish assembly, which enacted a series of savage anti-Catholic measures known as the Penal Code.

The 19th Century saw the terrible effects of the Great Famine (1845–48) when the potato crop on which the rural population depended was devastated by blight. Many people emigrated or died of starvation, and Ulster lost 500,000 of its population. The latter part of the century brought campaigns for national independence and land reform. A constitutional movement for Home Rule sought a separate Irish parliament, but this was not implemented until after World War I with the signing of the Anglo-Irish Treaty in 1921, ratified a year later. Under this, Northern Ireland had a regional parliament, based at Stormont near Belfast. The political unrest in the 1970s resulted in the suspension of Stormont, which was replaced by direct rule from Westminster.

Ulster has an extensive coastline and in the west the stormy Atlantic beats against the shores of Donegal. From Malin Head – Ireland's most northerly point – to Ballyshannon in the south, a mountain barrier shields the inland areas. Quarzite peaks such as Errigal and Muckish in the north, and Slieve League in the south, rise from a vast plateau. In some places this extends to the sea, forming lofty seascapes like Horn Head. The rugged coastline is softened by sandy beaches and huge bays like Ballyness.

Along the north Antrim coast the volcanic lava is underlaid with chalk, forming white cliffs, honeycombed with caves. In some places the sea's edge is chequered with white boulders and black basalts. This stretch of coast is called the Causeway Coast, being the site of Northern Ireland's well-known landmark. Giant's Causeway consists of about 37,000 hexagonal basaltic columns, closely

Giant's Causeway, County Antrim.

Above: *Newcastle Beach, dominated by the Mountains of Mourne, County Down.*
Right: *Dunluce Castle, County Antrim. Occupied until 1639 when part of it fell into the sea while the castle was full of guests.*

packed together at different heights. They form stepping stones from the base of the cliff which disappear into the sea. These were formed not, as claimed in the 19th Century, by a petrified bamboo forest, but by the cooling and shrinking of molten lava 60,000,000 years ago. Some distinctively shaped formations have been given names like Giant's Organ, The Wishing Chair and the Chimney Pots. It is a dramatic sight, whether lit by the setting sun or touched by a rainbow. Accessible now, it was a harder place to visit in the time of Dr Johnson, whose cryptic verdict was that it was 'worth seeing but not worth going to see'.

The east coast of Ulster is famous for its beautiful scenery, where wooded valleys cut through the Antrim Mountains down to the sea. The names of its nine glens each have a particular meaning, like Glenarm (glen of the army), Glencorp (glen of the slaughter) and Glentaise (Taisie's glen). In legend, Taisie was a princess from Rathlin Island who was fought over by a Viking and an Irish chief, and won by the Irishman.

Central Antrim, around Ballymena, is a fertile and prosperous farming region. Its prosperity is also due to the development of the linen industry in this area, begun in the 17th Century by Huguenot refugees who had sought sanctuary in Ulster. By the 19th Century there were numerous water-powered mills, dyeworks, bleachworks, weaving factories and beetling mills, remnants of which may still be found. The Lagan valley became important because of its access to the developing port of Belfast.

Only a village in the 17th Century, Belfast's population grew by leaps and bounds with the expansion of industries like cotton, linen, ropemaking, engineering and tobacco. By the 1880s its population had reached almost 300,000, and it was subsequently given city status by Queen Victoria. Belfast is ringed by hills – Black Mountain, Cavehill and Divis Mountain in the north and west and the Castlereagh Hills sloping down towards the gentler landscapes of County Down in the south. Out of the docks rise the spider-like gantries of giant cranes in the shipyards, which have held a world-wide reputation for shipbuilding since Harland and Wolff constructed their first all-iron ship in 1862.

Belfast is a compact city and its central area is easy to explore, from the impressive white

edifice of the City Hall to the mellow brick-work of Queen's University. In the almost unusual quietness of the city centre it is possible to remain quite unaware of the tension that exists between Protestants and Catholics on the surrounding estates.

South of Belfast, in County Down, are the famous Mountains of Mourne that 'sweep down to the sea'. Their imposing summits can be seen from miles around, and no road crosses over the central area. The Sperrin Mountains south of Derry are Northern Ireland's other great range, where 40 miles of gentler slopes run from east to west. Here, at Beaghmore, about a thousand stone-age standing stones appear like frozen figures scattered over a vast moor.

Ulster has other prehistoric landmarks; the burial cairns on many of its hilltops were originally erected over stone boxes containing human remains. But the main monument is the

Previous pages: *Sea anglers prepare to leave Ballintoy Harbour, County Antrim.*
Left: *Crown Bar, Belfast (National Trust).*
Right: *City Hall, Belfast, opened in 1906.*
Below: *Stormont, formerly the seat of the Northern Irish parliament.*

Below: *The 'Newton Window', a five-light transome window in Derry's Guildhall. The lower openings represent the Relief of Derry on 26 July 1869 after a 15-week siege.*

Above: *Enniskillen Castle, County Fermanagh.*
Right: *Florence Court, County Fermanagh. An 18th-Century mansion, it is in the care of the National Trust.*

great circular fort of Grianan of Aileach, near the border of Londonderry and Donegal, a famous royal cashel consisting of a series of defensive rings on an 800-foot hilltop.

In County Fermanagh, the long length of Upper and Lower Lough Erne covers over 50 miles, linked in the middle by the county town of Enniskillen. The lakeland is studded with islands, some of which, like Devenish Island and Boa Island, have interesting religious remains. On White Island eight mysterious

Right: *Rain descends on the Mourne Mountains, County Down.*
Opposite: *A donkey is still an important asset when it comes to collecting peat, as seen here on Horn Head, County Donegal.*
Below: *Glencolumbkille Folk Village, County Donegal.*

stone figures are set into the wall of a 12th-Century church. Although probably early Christian, several have a strange pagan look, which has resulted in a perpetual controversy over their origin.

Donegal is wilder and more remote than the other two Ulster provinces in the Irish Republic, Cavan and Monaghan. When the country was partitioned, Donegal was cut off from its port and focal point, the city of Derry, and in many ways it has remained less developed than its neighbour. As part of Britain, Northern Ireland has benefited from greater agricultural development and industrial investment.

There is a different feel to Northern Ireland that is experienced as soon as you cross the border. The landscape is generally more cultivated and, together with the type of housing built, is more reminiscent of England. Union Jacks hung out in Protestant areas emphasize this even further. Much of the countryside is attractively tranquil, but the fenced-off police stations, armoured cars and army patrols in major towns and cities are an uncomfortable reminder that this is a land of conflict as well as beauty.

Opposite: *View down Glenariff, one of the nine glens of County Antrim.*
Left: *An Ancient Janus figure found in Caldragh Cemetery, Boa Island, in Lower Lough Erne, County Fermanagh.*
Below: *Sheep Haven, County Donegal.*

Connaught

Connaught is perhaps the least accessible of Ireland's provinces, with its wild and remote areas of mountains, lakes and boglands. A relatively barren region, it is stunning in the sunshine and dramatic in dark clouds and brooding mountain mists. It is bounded by the River Shannon in the east, and the Atlantic coast in the west. Water dominates the terrain, from lakes of all sizes, through rivers and streams, to the wild beauty of the jagged coastline, with its long tongues of water probing deep inside the land.

Its uninviting shoreline and relatively infertile land deterred many early invaders. Although the Vikings entered the eastern part of Ireland in the 9th Century, they made few

Previous pages: View towards the Renvyle Peninsula, County Galway.
Opposite: A lough near Maam Cross, the crossroads between north and south Connemara, County Galway.
Below: Fishing in the rain on Kylemore Lough, County Galway.

attempts to occupy the northwest, or did not remain for long, and the tribes of Connaught were left largely to themselves.

When the Anglo-Normans did eventually take over the province, they still tended to avoid the far west, and Connaught stayed fairly unscathed by foreign influences for several centuries. When Cromwell and his New Model Army savagely crushed Irish resistance and drove many native landowners west in the mid-17th Century, 'To hell or Connaught' was their catchphrase for fleeing to the most barren region of the country.

Connaught suffered greatly in the Great Famine of the 1840s. Its land was hard to cultivate at the best of times, dependence on the normally hardy potato crop was great, and the potato blight took a heavy toll. Thousands died of starvation, and it is said that the Doo Lough Pass in County Mayo is haunted at night by the many people who died at the wayside walking down to seek food. The province was further depopulated by families who decided to brave the journey to a new

world and sailed for North America rather than face the prospect of starvation at home.

Although the rocky, infertile terrain deterred migrants from settling on the land, the region did attract religious individuals and communities seeking isolation and asceticism. The many ecclesiastical remains found on off-shore islands and on remote parts of the coast provide evidence of their hard and primitive way of life. West of the Mullet peninsula in County Mayo lie several uninhabited islands which were once great monastic centres, such as Inishglora and Inishkea. Inishmurray, off the coast of County Sligo, has a well-preserved early Irish monastery. One of the small churches is named 'the Men's Church' and had a burial ground for men only. Tradition held that if a woman was buried there, the body would be miraculously transferred to 'The Women's Church', situated in another area of the grounds.

Religious sites still attract thousands of people on pilgrimages. Croagh Patrick in County Mayo is a famous holy mountain with

a glittering quartzite cone. St Patrick is supposed to have climbed to the top to fast for the 40 days of Lent. Myths have grown up around his stay, including the creation of nearby Lough Nacorra by his hurling a demon from the mountainside, which thereby banished all venomous creatures from Ireland. Every last Sunday in July, countless people repeat his climb, some with bare feet.

The village of Knock, also in County Mayo, is a more recent focus for pilgrims. In 1879 local inhabitants claimed to have seen an apparition of three figures, the central one identified as the Blessed Virgin. A Commission of Enquiry held that it was genuine, and it was formally recognized as a Marian shrine, and visited by the Pope in 1979.

Croagh Patrick stands high over Clew Bay, which is strewn with little islands called drumlins, mounds of sand and gravel squeezed from the base of an advancing ice sheet during the Ice Age. In the 16th Century this area of the coast was the haunt of a legendary pirate and sea-captain, Grace O'Malley.

Left: *The rather dilapidated* Casablanca, *moored on a lough near Letterfrack, County Galway.*
Below: *In contrast, the traditional currach, the smallest of these boats moored in Killary Harbour, County Galway, is still well-used by local fishermen.*

The most well-known islands along the Connaught coast are the Aran Islands – Inishmore, Inishmaan, and Inisheer – in the mouth of Galway Bay. They are a bastion of Irish language and custom and the inhabitants follow a traditional lifestyle which attracts many tourists. These islands have been inhabited for a long time. According to the ancient *Annals of the Four Masters* they were the scene of a battle documented as taking place in the 303rd year of the world. St Enda, who is responsible for introducing the monastic tradition to Ireland in the 5th Century, founded a settlement on the islands which has left a rich collection of remains. The island people needed strong powers of survival. On the stony, soilless limestone outcrops that make up most of the islands they carefully fertilized the small wall-edged fields with sand and seaweed until they had enough for potatoes, oats and some grass for the cattle. Fishing was skilfully carried out in currachs, frail canvas-covered canoes. Currachs are still used, although now there is also a modern trawler fleet.

Many deep coastal inlets form long harbours, boring into the land. One such is beautiful Killary Harbour. Dividing Galway and Mayo, it is lined with mountains including the great Mweelrea, which rises starkly from the water's edge. The calm water is dotted with mussel rafts; the cultivation of this

shellfish is becoming a thriving new industry. Streams and rivers find their way to the sea from the numerous inland loughs, the high gradients forming waterfalls which cascade down the mountainsides, especially after a rainstorm. Lower down on the River Erriff, a torrent of water thunders over Aasleagh Falls, a prospect that does not seem to daunt the intrepid trout and salmon trying to make their way upstream to the spawning grounds.

The water at Aasleagh Falls is coloured yellow-brown by the bogland areas through which it has travelled. These areas provide an important source of fuel, the cut peat is used both for domestic fires and in power stations. Over much of this region mounds of cut turf are a common sight. They are stacked to dry next to the waterlogged pits from where they are dug, the walls of which are patterned herringbone-fashion by the slanting cuts of a single-edged 'slane'. Nearby, the white fluffy heads of the bog cotton plant blow in the breeze.

While the Connaught coast is enlivened by many islands, the land is full of lakes. The River Shannon, which divides the province from Leinster, broadens out into lakes in several places. The largest is Lough Derg, whose northern and western shores lie in County Galway. In the south of Galway, Lough Rea is sprinkled with crannogs, ancient stockaded islands built by early lake dwellers who looked to water not only for food but also for defence.

Lough Corrib, to the east of the province, is a very popular fishing centre, and the pleasant town of Oughterard has been playing host to optimistic anglers for 150 years. At its northern tip, Lough Corrib is only a couple of miles from the southern shore of another large lough, Lough Mask. In the 19th Century, a project was undertaken to link the two by a canal, duly completed in 1850. But engineers had not accounted for the porous limestone and as soon as the water flowed into the canal it vanished from sight! The connecting strip of land is a strategic location, and the site of Cong Abbey there was once occupied by the ancient Kings of Connaught.

Left: *Clifden, perched above an inlet of Ardbear Bay, is regarded by many as the capital of Connemara.*
Below: *Ellen's Pub, County Sligo.*

Above: *Doo Lough Pass, County Mayo.*
Left: *Trout fishing at Aasleagh Falls, County Mayo.*

The principal city in the west of Ireland is Galway, which lies between Lough Corrib and the sea. It was an important medieval trading post and in the 15th Century, when a brisk trade had developed with Spain, Richard II of England granted a charter which made the town into a city state. This dispossessed the local ruling family, the de Burgos, who consequently harassed the city, but the greatest threat came from the O'Flahertys, who ruled the entire territory of West Connaught until the end of the 16th Century. So terrified of them were the people of Galway that they had an inscription written over the west gate of the town that said, 'From the ferocious O'Flahertys Good Lord deliver us'.

Galway was taken by Williamite forces at the end of the 17th Century, after which the city declined in importance. In the 19th

Century it became a university city and also the centre for a reawakening of interest in Ireland's Celtic past, with the formation of the Gaelic League in 1893. This was an important source for the ideas of the Irish revolution which ultimately led to the establishment of the Irish Free State in 1922. Today Irish language, culture and literary heritage still flourish in much of County Galway.

Part of Ireland's literary heritage comes from the poet W B Yeats, who used to spend boyhood holidays near Lough Gill in County Sligo, in northern Connaught. This area inspired much of his poetry, and is revisited repeatedly in his words and imagery. 'The Lake Isle of Innisfree' and 'The Fiddler of Dooney' are two well-known examples. Yeats was buried at Drumcliff, north of Sligo Town in 1939, and the plain limestone slab on his grave bears the lines he wrote in anticipation of his death:

> Cast a cold eye
> On life, on death.
> Horseman, pass by!

Rising above rivers and lakes are the craggy and striking mountains that cover the western part of the prvince. The giant altar-like form of Benbulben looms over the northern part of County Sligo, with its velvety green folds. To its west is Knocknarra mountain, on the summit of which is a gigantic cairn, supposedly the tomb of the legendary Queen Maeve, the 1st-Century ruler of Connaught. On a fine day it affords magnificent views to the Ox Mountains in the south and the mountains of Donegal to the north.

Galway has several distinctive mountain ranges. The Twelve Pins dominate Connemara in the west of the county. Northeast of these, the Maumturks form a long line, flanked in the east by Joyce's Country. The sparsely

Below: After a storm, water races down to Killary Harbour, County Galway.

populated area of northwest Mayo contains Nephin Beg and other jagged peaks, to form some of the wildest and loveliest country in the whole of Ireland.

The counties of Roscommon and Leitrim are less mountainous. Leitrim is divided by

Previous pages: *A view of the Twelve Pins, County Galway.*
Opposite: *Kylemore Abbey, County Galway. Built by Mitchell Henry in 1864 for his wife, it now houses a convent school run by Benedictine Nuns.*
Below: *Aughnanure Castle, Oughterard, County Galway. A stronghold of the fierce O'Flahertys where, the story goes, a trap door in the banqueting hall released offending visitors into the river below.*

Lough Allen, and the north and south regions are quite distinct. In the northern part of the long thin county, a series of table mountains are separated by spectacular valleys such as Glencar, with the Iron Mountains rising up to the east of the lough. In the south however, the terrain is much flatter and covered by low, rounded hillocks.

Roscommon is an inland county and possesses the most fertile land in the province. It is also a fisherman's paradise, with its limestone foundation and many lakes. Two-thirds of the county is bounded by water and a third is bogland. The rich arable land in the centre made it one of the first areas populated by foreign invaders, and Rathcroghan, in the centre, was a home of the kings of Connaught and later of the High Kings of Ireland.

There is a sense of freedom in Connaught's wild countryside, and an exhilaration gained from high mountains and long fjord-like valleys and vast moorland bogs. Small villages nestle here and there, farmhouses are scattered around, and stone-built towns like Clifden in the heart of Connemara have a traditional charm. Sheep graze over the mountain slopes. In Killary Harbour they come down to the sea's edge when the tide is out to eat the seaweed. In the north of the province, telephone conversation is achieved by turning the winders on old-fashioned black phones, which miraculously crackle into life as the operator answers. It is a region that retains its traditions, its people are warm and welcoming, and life proceeds at a leisurely and civilized pace while the modern world rushes by.

Left, above and below: *Views along the Doo Lough Pass, County Mayo.*

Above: *Kylemore Lough, County Galway, with the Maumturk Mountains in the distance.*
Left: *Belbulben towers over the countryside in County Sligo.*
Below: *Croagh Patrick, the 'Holy Mountain' in County Mayo.*

Dublin

Dublin is for many a favourite city, with its charming mixture of elegance and dilapidation, and the friendly warmth of its people. Protected by the beautiful Howth peninsula in the north and the rocky coastline to Killiney in the south, it lies at the head of Dublin Bay. Midway down the country's east coast, Dublin's accessibility has lent strategic importance, and as Ireland's central seat of government it has witnessed many momentous events.

The city is divided in two by the legendary River Liffey, which flows through the docks, alongside the elegant façades of the Custom House and the Four Courts, beneath the shadow of Christchurch Cathedral and the Guinness brewery, past the vast green expanse of Phoenix Park and into the countryside. Although nearly a third of the Irish Republic's population, almost 1,000,000 people, live in Dublin, the city is not large. It is quite easy to wander around the centre, taking a stroll over the curve of fragile Halfpenny Bridge and along the river, down through the cobbled quadrangles of Trinity College, up through the colourful bustle of shoppers in Grafton Street, and into leafy St Stephen's Green. The city's many historic buildings, parks, shops and bars attract an invasion of visitors, some of whom come simply to admire, while others come to visit relatives and discover lost roots.

Dublin's invaders have not always been so well-intentioned. The Norsemen who arrived in the 9th Century were setting up ports for inland plunder all over the European coast. They established Dublin as a garrison town and a trading post. From then on, it remained in foreign hands, except briefly in 1014 when warrior-king Brian Boru rallied the Irish to defeat the Vikings at Clontarf, just outside Dublin, and then drove them out of the city.

The Norman invasion of Ireland began in 1169, after Dermot MacMurrough, banished king of Leinster, sought help in England from Henry II. Dublin was the ideal location for their headquarters, close to the British coast and already well-developed as a naval port by

Previous pages: *View over Dublin from the top of Liberty Hall.*
Opposite: *The O'Connell Bridge over the River Liffey, Dublin.*
Above: *A crowd of umbrellas jostle on Halfpenny Bridge while* (below) *night brings a more tranquil view.*

the Vikings. Thus began Ireland's long and troubled association with England.

It was in this period that Dublin took its name. Originally the surrounding area of land was very swampy and unpopulated, until a marauding northern king, returning from a raid on Leinster, built a hurdle bridge over the River Liffey. The land around began to be colonized and was known as Baile Ath A Chath, the Town of the Hurdle Ford. Subsequently the Irish changed it to Duibhlinn, or Dark Pool, from the dark-brown-coloured water of the Liffey. The Norsemen called it Dyfflin and the Anglo-Normans Dublinne, from which its present name is derived.

The Normans rapidly dominated about three-quarters of the country, but over the

45

years they were gradually assimilated into the local population. Although they succeeded in establishing a system of parliament, law and administration in Ireland based on that in England, by the end of the 15th Century the area of Norman rule had been reduced to a narrow strip of land on the east coast, to the north and south of Dublin, known as the 'English Pale', or the 'Obedient Shires'. The Tudor monarchs set out to remedy this situation with a series of military campaigns against the Gaelic Irish and lapsed Anglo-Norman lords. Irish Catholic support for the Royalists in the English Civil War resulted in the decimation of the Catholic population, their lands were taken away and given to English Protestant settlers. These Anglo-Irish became the landlords of Ireland, with Dublin as their capital. Catholics were left as tenant farmers with little security and a low standard of living. By the 18th Century they had been excluded from parliament and deprived of their rights.

At the same time as they were relentlessly persecuting the Catholic population, the ascendant Protestants were providing many of Dublin's greatest buildings. One of the earliest,

begun in 1729 by Sir Edward Lovett Pearse, housed the Irish parliament. It was added to over the next 70 years, and after the 1800 Act of Union, was taken over by the Bank of Ireland, who still occupy it today. Its tall white colonnades sweep majestically round College Green, the east side of which is taken up with another beautiful piece of architecture, Trinity College, Dublin's foremost university.

Trinity's dark-grey façade surrounds several attractive quadrangles, and contains the University of Dublin, founded in 1592 by Elizabeth I. Along one side of a grassy quadrangle is the Old Library, the most famous part of which is the Long Room. The mellow browns of centuries-old books and manuscripts and the polished wooden bookcases give the Long Room a very special atmosphere

Opposite: *Grafton Street, Dublin's main shopping thoroughfare.*
Right: *The modern style of the Bank of Ireland in Baggott Street has caused much controversy among those who favour the more classical lines of the older Bank in College Green* (below).

Above and below: *Doheny and Nesbitt, a popular bar with the legal profession.*
Below right: *The decorative interior of The Long Hall typifies many of Dublin's bars.*
Opposite: *St Patrick's Cathedral, one of Dublin's two Protestant cathedrals.*

of cool tranquillity. Its most treasured possession is the Book of Kells, one of the most beautifully illuminated manuscripts in the world, dating from about AD 800. It contains the Latin text of the Four Gospels, illustrated with pages of intricate paintings as well as smaller painted decorations throughout the fine script. The library's calm presence is so effective that a college librarian even admitted that if ever things got on top of her, 'I just go to the Long Room and look at the Book of Kells and everything's alright again'.

Many other fine buildings were constructed during this era, such as the Royal Exchange, the Custom House and the Four Courts on the north bank of the river. New, spacious streets and squares appeared, whose names still recall the wealthy speculators responsible for them, such as Fitzwilliam, Molesworth and Herbert. These elegant Georgian terraces, with their wide, brightly painted doorways and ivy-clad walls, still mark the wealthier area of the city today.

The 18th Century thus saw a transformation in Dublin City. The settler landlords made the land more productive by introducing new farming methods, exports of meat, dairy and linen increased, and the capital became rich on the profits from the countryside. The city ranked second in the British Empire. Many landlords lived in their magnificent Palladian houses in Dublin and appointed managers to run their rural estates. Country people, however, were getting poorer, with higher rents, fewer jobs and a rising birthrate, and the illusion of opportunity brought them flocking to the city.

Although Irish Catholics made up over half the population, they had little part in the progress of the 18th Century. Some succeeded in trading activities, and adopted the attitudes of the dominant Protestants. They were known as 'Castle Catholics', because of their deference to English rule. Dublin Castle was the stronghold of English rule in Ireland from the mid-13th Century. The castle's rambling courtyards were built in an assortment of styles by a succession of viceroys, and its gilt-painted, chandeliered and lushly furnished staterooms were the scene of numerous high-society dances, dinners and concerts. At the annual St Patrick's Ball, the viceroy bestowed knighthoods and received new debutantes into court circles. But for Catholics and poorer Protestants, the Castle was a symbol of British imperial power, whose methods of suppressing dissent were much feared.

It was Daniel O'Connell, a Catholic barrister, who was to change this situation. He formed the Catholic Association in 1823 to campaign for full religious freedom. This rapidly became a mass movement and successfully forced the London parliament to grant Catholic Emancipation in 1829. He is remembered in Dublin by the wide central avenue and bridge named after him, and by the O'Connell Monument.

O'Connell Street is also famous as the site of the Easter Rising of 1916, when a group of men from Ireland's two unofficial armies, the Irish Volunteers and the Irish Citizen Army, took over the General Post Office Building. Shortly afterwards, Patrick Pearse, a leading Irish Volunteer, emerged into the fine Ionic portico to read a proclamation for Free Ireland and the formation of a provisional government of the Irish Republic. With him was James Connolly, the commander of the Irish Citizen Army. They and five other signatories of the proclamation had been planning the uprising for many months, as the climax of their struggle to free the country from British rule. Their initial achievement was sadly short-lived. Subsequent fighting with British soldiers only lasted about a week before the rebels were completely outnumbered and Pearse and Connolly forced into unconditional surrender. They were tried and shot with 13 other rebel leaders a month later. In military terms, the uprising had not been very successful, but it did serve to precipitate feelings and events that contributed towards the war of independence that culminated in the signing of the Anglo-Irish Treaty in 1921. The country was by no means content, however, and the two years of Anglo-Irish war preceding the Treaty were followed by two years of Irish civil war over its terms. After 1922, Dublin grew

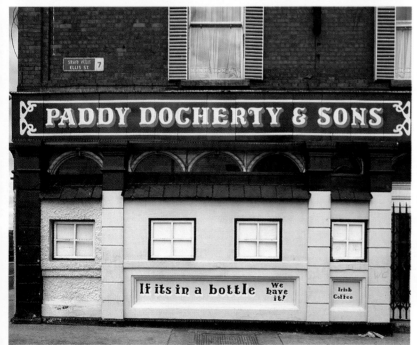

slowly, suffering the long economic recession until the 1960s, when economic expansion brought increasing development and consequent growth in employment. Nowadays, modern architecture stands, sometimes rather uneasily, next to the classical grandeur of the 18th Century.

The ruling Protestants always had a keen enthusiasm for literature, music and theatre. In 1742, the composer Handel was invited to Dublin by the English viceroy, where he composed his *Messiah*. Ireland has produced a wealth of literary talent, such as 18th Century authors Jonathan Swift, Oliver Goldsmith and Richard Brinsley Sheridan; Oscar Wilde and Bernard Shaw in the 19th Century; followed by the flourishing of an Irish literary Renaissance in the 20th Century, a few of whose contributors are William Butler Yeats, James Joyce, Sean O'Casey, Brendan Behan, Samuel Beckett and Mary Lavin.

Religion has always been central to Irish history and politics. Although the centre of a major Catholic diocese, it is significant that

Previous pages: *A few of Dublin's many and varied bars.*
Opposite: *The Long Room in the Old Library of Trinity College contains the beautifully illustrated* Book of Kells.
Right and below: *The grounds and Halls of Residence of Trinity College, Dublin.*

Dublin has no Catholic cathedral but two Protestant cathedrals, St Patrick's and Christchurch, both built in the 13th Century. St Patrick's was built by Archbishop Comyn, a Norman baron, in a vain effort to supercede Christchurch Cathedral, erected by St Lorcan O'Toole. After the Reformation both were placed under the Protestant Church of Ireland. The celebrated Jonathan Swift was Dean of St Patrick's from 1713 to 1745.

While religious activities take an important role, a crucial part of Dublin life is carried out in its countless bars, which serve as meeting places for business, gossip, courtship or simply to savour a quiet glass of guinness. Traditional Irish music is played in bars such as O'Donahue's, either by arrangement or with a delightful spontaneity.

Many bars are decorated with eye-catching mirror-work, both inside and out, together with elegant stained glass and polished woodwork, as in The Long Hall bar. In some, like Doheny and Nesbitt, where the legal profession drink, discreet cubicles allow their occupants to discuss intimate topics out of public view. Others have achieved fame because of the people who used to frequent them; James Joyce, for instance, featured various of Dublin's bars in his writings. It is said that Brendan Behan knew all the bars in the city, but the one he knew the best was McDaid's, where he set his typewriter and glass in a corner and worked on his plays. Yeats, on the other hand, is said to have made only one visit to a pub, where after drinking a glass of sherry he said, 'I have seen a pub now. Will you kindly take me home.'

The drink to savour in Dublin is not sherry however, but smooth black stout. The city is the home of the Guinness brewery, where visitors can admire the result of a fortunate accident. The story goes that in 1759 a struggling young brewer called Arthur Guinness happened to burn the wort and hops, and gave away the offending product for nothing. To his surprise his customers returned next day asking for more. Whether true or not, he began brewing his 'porter' in the Rainsford Brewery and the family fortune was made. The power of Guinness is well summed up by Flann O'Brien in 'The Workman's Friend', from his novel, *At-Swim-Two-Birds*:

Previous pages: Elegant Georgian doorways are a feature of Dublin's streets and squares.
Left: The Grand Canal runs all the way from Dublin through County Kildare to the River Shannon.
Below: Joyce's Tower, Sandycove. James Joyce stayed briefly in this Martello tower in 1904 and it features in his novel Ulysses.

When things go wrong and will not come
 right
Though you do the best you can,
When life looks black as the hour of night –
A PINT OF PLAIN IS YOUR ONLY
 MAN...

The province of Munster in the southwest has some of the finest scenery in the country. It covers nearly 10,000 square miles, and has an extensive coastline that runs along the edge of counties Waterford, Cork, Kerry, Limerick and Clare. Tipperary is the only county that is landlocked. Around the coast, mountains, rivers, rocky cliffs, sandy bays and muddy estuaries intermingle to form an ever-changing landscape. The south-west peninsulas attract a host of visitors, drawn to justifiably well-known places such as Bantry Bay, the Lakes of Killarney, the Beara Peninsula, and the Ring of Kerry.

Munster's horizons always seem quite close because there are few areas that are not dominated by mountains. Ranges like the Slieve Felims, Silvermines and Galties run inland, while on the coast, clusters of peaks crowd into long promontories and tower over rocky bays. Mountains play an important role in defining county boundaries. The stern Knockmealdown Mountains separate Tipperary from Waterford, reached by a jack-knife road called 'The Vee', which provides commanding views over slopes of wild rhododendron bushes towards the Golden Vale. The boundary between Cork and Kerry on the road from Glengarriff to Kenmare goes through the 'tunnels' road, where the contemporary traveller drives easily through Turner's Rock in the Caha Mountains. In Victorian times it was a more difficult prospect, and passengers had to wait for their vehicles to be carried over the top on the shoulders of men from the surrounding countryside.

The peninsulas in the south-west of the province possess some of the highest mountains in the country. Macgillycuddy's Reeks, near the Killarney Lakes in County Kerry, culminate in lofty Carrauntuohill, which at 3400 feet is the highest peak in Ireland. The Slieve Mish Mountains run all the way down to the tip of the Dingle Peninsula. The Beara

Previous pages: *Slea Head, Dingle Peninsula, County Kerry.*
Left: *The herringbone pattern created by peat cutting provides an attractive backdrop for the bog cotton plant.*
Below: *Traditional farm implements are still found throughout the Irish Republic.*

Peninsula is made up of the Slieve Miskish and Caha ranges, crossed from north to south by the Healy Pass, which winds precariously up the steep inclines.

These ranges were shaped by the movement of giant glaciers during the Ice Age. Long channels of ice were forced through river valleys and through cracks in hills, creating lakes, corries, and 'gaps' like the well-trodden Gap of Dunloe that runs through the Macgillycuddy Reeks. Nearby, the Killarney Valley and its three famous lakes provide memorable landscapes such as 'The Ladies View', supposedly named after the appreciation it evoked from Queen Victoria's ladies-in-waiting when they stopped there over a

Previous pages: The whole family still works in the fields at haymaking time.
Opposite: Rugged country near Sneem, County Kerry.
Right: Haymaking near Dingle Bay, County Kerry.
Below: The local blacksmith practises his skill in Ennistymon, County Clare.

century ago. Such views, as with many others in Ireland, are subject to the rapidly changing weather conditions. The vibrant hues of blue skies and sea, green hills and valleys, brilliant in the sun, can simply dissolve away into a grey mist in which peaks and other contours vanish into a monochrome curtain of rain, or become dramatic and ominous with a mixture of bright light and brooding black cloud.

The countryside in Munster has many small details to charm the passing traveller. Roadside verges are covered with small, brightly coloured flowers, mixed up with wild dog roses and honeysuckle in the summer months. The climate in this area is almost always mild, encouraging the growth of subtropical trees and shrubs, which mingle with bright-red fuchsia bushes. There are tiny whitewashed houses, thatched barns, precarious hillside farms, villages with stone-washed houses in delicate pastel shades, isolated gothic farmhouses, desolate ruined castles and abandoned stone houses. Long bricks of cut peak stand propped up against each other to dry in bogland areas. In July the fields are dotted with

haystacks, whose construction may have the whole family working to turn the hay and make the familiar yellow mounds. Sights like this, together with shepherds herding their flocks and horses and donkeys pulling carts, are reminders of a different pace of life, where farming still depends as much on labour as machinery.

In these areas, the unhurried atmosphere is complemented by the open friendliness of the local people. On the relatively empty roads, drivers give and receive cheery waves of acknowledgement from anyone walking or working along the roadside. In the local bars, intense conversation and lively music may go on well into the night. Music is a very important part of Irish culture, and both the merry sounds of a group of musicians and the

haunting refrain sung by an unaccompanied voice express a deep wealth of history as well as emotion. History survives too in the celebration of old traditions. In Dingle, for example, 26 December is the Day of the Wren, when everyone dresses up and parades round the streets wearing masks. A few selected people wear special straw suits and pointed straw hats – these are the Wren Boys. The custom derives from the idea that it was a wren that betrayed Christ, and the aim is to hunt it down.

Material evidence of Ireland's history is also found throughout the countryside; the province is a treasure trove of ancient remains. Near Glandore, a pretty harbour village in Cork, the 17 stones which form the Drombeg stone circle have stood erect for thousands of years since the Megalithic Period. The region has numerous stone forts, but the most sophisticated is Staigue Fort in Kerry, which has a finely preserved circular wall and elaborate staircases. In medieval times a great many castles were built for defence, and by the 16th

Century most of Munster's coast was guarded by such fortressed buildings. These were often constructed on exposed rocks, as is Dunlochy Castle at Mizen Head, which dominates the horizons at the top of a 300-foot cliff. Many others, mainly tower houses, are still found scattered around the countryside in various states of preservation. They were used as dwelling places as well as fortresses, the top floor being the home of the castle lord and his family. Today it is hard to imagine ever being warm and comfortable in such basic surroundings.

The ingeniously constructed beehive huts on the Iveragh and Dingle Peninsulas are good examples of dry-rubble masonry, built by the inhabitants of early Christian monasteries. The Gallarus Oratory represents an extremely well-preserved example, dating from around the 8th Century. It is incredible to realize that the builders, without mortar, managed to create a perfectly balanced curved roof out of heavy stone, which has survived intact for over a thousand years to delight the beholder today.

Previous pages: *Upper Lake Killarney, County Kerry.*
Below: *The stern profile of the Cliffs of Moher, County Clare, contrasts with the gentler lines of Cumeenoole Strand, County Kerry* (right).

Many churches and hermit's cells are found in coastal places, reflecting an early Christian desire to pursue religion through asceticism and contemplation of the sea. On the largest of the Skellig Islands, which lie eight miles off the Iveragh Peninsula, an early Christian community seeking such solitude built its stone huts and oratories near the mountain summit.

Previous pages: *Glandore Harbour, County Cork.*
Far right: *Poulnadrome Dolmen, standing on the cracked limestone pavement of The Burren, County Clare.*
Below right: *The perfectly preserved 8th-Century Gallarus Oratory, County Kerry.*
Below: *Timoleague Abbey, on the edge of Courtmacsherry Bay, County Cork.*

On the south coast of Cork the picturesque ruins of Timoleague Abbey, at the head of Courtmacsherry Bay, also illustrates this preferred location.

Perhaps the greatest collection of ancient ruins stands majestically on the Rock of Cashel in Tipperary, which rises steeply above the rich pasture of the Golden Vale. The name cashel derives from the Latin *castellum* (castle), and this fortress site was known as the Castle of the Kings. Here the early kings of Munster reigned from at least the 5th Century until the time of Brian Boru in the 11th Century. In 1101, Muirchertach O'Brien handed Cashel over to the church, thereby transferring it from a royal seat to an episcopal one. Its interesting medieval buildings include St Cormac's Chapel, built by a king-bishop in 1127. It

stands snugly in the corner of the cathedral, built at a later date, and is decorated with the finely carved heads of humans and animals. The Rock of Cashel dominates the surrounding countryside and presents an awesome sight, both by day and silhouetted by night.

Most of Munster's coastline is exposed to the wild elements of the Atlantic Ocean. The more sheltered nature of the south is reflected in the gentle shores of Waterford County with its sandy bays and miles of cliffs. The southeast coast of Cork has a series of natural harbours, such as at Kinsale. This attractive town is most famous for the battle in which Hugh O'Neill and Red Hugh O'Donnell, the Earl of Tyrone and Lord of Tyrconnel, supported by Spanish forces, were defeated by the English on Christmas Day 1601.

In southwest Cork and Kerry, centuries of wind, rain and sea have torn the coast into jagged strips of land that stretch like ragged ribbons into the sea. Many a boat has been broken up after being blown on to the lethal rocky headlands. Further north, in County Clare, the towering cliffs of Moher present a dramatic and dangerous profile from both land and sea. At the top, a 19th-Century folly called O'Brien's Tower was built for the benefit of visitors overcome by feelings of vertigo at the 700-foot view to the rocks below.

The constant battering of the ocean against the coast has formed craggy cliffs and a scattering of off-shore islands. Some of these have been inhabited until quite recently, such as the Blasket Islands, off Dingle Peninsula, which were finally abandoned in 1953. Many

islands that are untouched by man are populated by birds. Little Skellig and Bull Island, for instance, are the homes of thousands of gannets. The Great Skellig also has kittiwakes, guillemots, petrel, shearwater and fulmar, and on a calm day, large drifts of these can be seen on the surface of the sea. Puffin Island, off the Iveragh Peninsula, is a breeding sanctuary for these attractive little birds.

Fishing has always been important here for survival and as a means of earning an income. In addition to the more common varieties of sea fish, such as herring, cod, whiting and mackerel, inland fishing provides a lot of salmon. Some of this is smoked and sent all over the world. The smoking process is done inside a kiln; the smoke from burning oak sawdust circulates around the fish for 10 to 12 hours to provide its distinctive flavour. On certain parts of the coast fishermen still use the small, black tar-painted currachs, the skilful handling of which is also demonstrated in local currach races.

As well as fishing, the smaller south-west ports and harbours are historically associated with piracy and smuggling. Dutch pirates used to anchor near the remote village of Schull in Cork ready to pounce on unsuspecting boats from the East India Fleet, and the Beara Peninsula and the north shore of the Kenmare River were centres for contraband trading in the 18th Century.

The southern areas of Waterford, and east Cork have larger urban centres and more small industries compared with the rural and remote western region. One of Waterford's best-known assets is its glassmaking industry, which originated in 1783. This not only provides a great source of local employment, but some of the finest cut glass in the world. Skilled cutters learn how to produce some 50 different patterns by heart. A small team of engravers work on specially commissioned pieces, whose intricate details take many hours to complete.

Munster province offers many kinds of landscapes and coastal scenery, from the undulating lowlands of Waterford and Limerick to the endless mountain horizons of Kerry and west Cork. In County Clare in the north, the dry, flat, limestone rocks and pavements of

Below and right: *The Beara Peninsula seen in the early evening light.*

the Burren present a moonscape of white-grey, full of caves and vanishing streams. Standing starkly in the middle of this is the Poulnadrome Dolmen, a striking stone table covering a 4000-year-old grave. Also on the Burren is a rare collection of Alpine-Arctic flora, a legacy of the Ice Age. This region of surprising contrasts and great beauty never fails to provide visual satisfaction.

Opposite: This ruined castle near Ballyneety, County Limerick, now provides local cattle with a stately shelter.
Right: The well-preserved walls of Staigue Fort, County Kerry, which protected humans and cattle from attack nearly 1000 years ago.
Below: The majestic Rock of Cashel, County Tipperary, crowning the hilltop, was the seat of the early kings of Munster.

Leinster presents a soft contrast to the aggressive contours of the Munster landscape. Although it has its share of hills and mountains, its long golden beaches and the low central limestone plain bestow a different aspect. The inland regions are comparatively highly populated, cultivated and forested, since accessible and fertile farmlands and a sunnier climate have attracted many settlers. The gentleness of the east coast has always lent an easy entry to adventurous invaders.

Previous pages: View towards the Blackstairs Mountains from County Kilkenny.
Opposite: Powerscourt Waterfall, County Wicklow, cascades from a height of almost 400 feet into the River Dargle.
Below: Johnstown Castle, County Wexford, now houses an agricultural research centre and museum.

Wexford's beaches in the south have seen many famous landings. St Patrick's arrival in AD 432, which brought Christianity, was made at the mouth of the River Boyne in County Louth.

Northern and central counties such as Louth, Meath, Westmeath and Longford are relatively flat, and in north Kildare and Offaly, a vast area of bogland stretches to the River Shannon. Further south, the appearance of the Slieve Bloom Mountains, shared by both Offaly and Laois creates a pleasant contrast. This range is a conspicuous feature of central Ireland. Further east, between Carlow and Wexford, the Blackstairs Mountains with Mount Leinster offer another striking profile. The Wicklow Mountains to the south of Dublin rise as massive peat-covered granite domes, forming a 40-mile chain that extends to the foothills of County Wexford. They were

used as a refuge by a large number of rebels at the end of the 18th Century and in order to flush them out the British built a great military road running north to south.

The Wicklow Mountains are broken by deep valleys and gorges, covered with moorland heather and crossed with streams and waterfalls. The wild beauty of the Vale of Glendalough (the valley of the two lakes) is heightened by a cluster of ancient religious buildings. An almost perfectly preserved round tower over 100-feet high, rises imposingly above the trees in the middle of a site where St Kevin founded a monastery in the 6th Century. It gained a high reputation as a centre of learning, and the ruined church, cathedral and other structures in this evocative setting exert a very strong presence.

Remains of an age when the Celtic church was flourishing can be found all over Leinster,

as at Monasterboice, Mellifont and Kells in the north. At Jerpoint Abbey in Kilkenny a 15th-Century cloister arcade still exhibits many fine carvings, from bishops and abbots to grotesque figures. The High Cross of Moone, thought to date from the 8th Century, stands tall and mysterious in the graveyard near a small village in Kildare. Its intricate stone-carving, depicting scenes such as Daniel in the lions' den, are strong and clear.

Left: *Glendalough, County Wicklow. These round towers were not only defensive but also were used as bell towers in early Irish monasteries to summon monks to prayer.*
Below: *The fine Hiberno-Romanesque doorway of Killoshin Church in County Laois is virtually the only remaining feature of the 6th-Century monastery.*

Perhaps the most celebrated of all Ireland's holy places is at Clonmacnoise in Offaly, where St Ciaran founded a monastery in the 6th Century. It was the burial place for kings, including the last High King of Ireland, Rory O'Connor, buried there in 1198. Surrounded by bog and bounded by the River Shannon, the site is a perfect example of the desire of monks to combine isolation with fertile land to work. The location was not inaccessible however, and as well as the students who travelled there from all over Europe, it was visited by the plundering forces of both Norsemen and native Irish, and almost totally destroyed by the English garrison from Athlone in 1552. Today the remains of its round towers, high crosses, cathedral and castle, next to the still waters of the Shannon, leave a memorable impression.

Previous pages: *A panoramic view of Enniscorthy and the River Slaney, County Wexford, seen from Vinegar Hill.*
Above: *All eyes right at The Curragh as the horses in the big race, the Irish Sweeps Derby, approach the winning post.*
Left: *The parade ring at the Curragh racecourse, County Kildare, where racegoers gain a closer view of their selections.*
Below: *A mare and her foal at the Irish National Stud, Tully, County Kildare.*

Leinster has played a significant part in Anglo-Irish history. At the beginning of the 11th Century, when Brian Boru became High King of Ireland, the MacMurroughs – kings of Leinster – resented the allegiance he demanded and joined with the Vikings to overthrow him. At the Battle of Clontarf in 1014 they were beaten, and this marked the end of Viking power in Ireland. The MacMurroughs continued as kings of Leinster, reluctantly supporting subsequent High Kings. When in 1166

Rory O'Connor recaptured the High Kingship, he expelled Dermot MacMurrough from the province who sought aid from Henry II in England. This resulted in the Norman invasion of Ireland in 1167, and the establishment of English rule.

In the 14th Century Art MacMurrough Kavannagh was king of Leinster and he was the scourge of the English armies in Ireland. His forces attacked the 'English Pale' so ferociously that Richard II was compelled to come over himself to try and quell them. His efforts were twice unsuccessful, first in 1394, and then in 1399. This second absence from

England, as portrayed in Shakespeare's famous play, was to cost him his throne.

The county of Kilkenny has its own share of history. This long, sword-shaped county has variously belonged to Munster and Leinster. Many early Normans settled here, attracted by its rich soils and forests. They and the native Irish rapidly intermingled, becoming, as the saying goes, 'more Irish than the Irish'. The assimilation was so complete that it caused great concern in London, resulting in a series of laws called the Statutes of Kilkenny in 1336. These created a form of apartheid by which it became high treason for, for example, an Anglo-Norman man to marry an Irish woman. Threatening as they sounded, the laws proved unenforceable, especially as by

this time most people were already a mixture of Irish and Norman.

Kilkenny City is nicknamed 'The Marble City' on account of its limestone rock which, when polished, turns as black as ink. Its fine castle stands impressively reflected in the protecting moat of the River Nore. As well as featuring in Irish history, Kilkenny has achieved a reputation in the indigenous game of hurling. This 15-a-side game dates back 2000 years. The ball is hit or carried through the air with a curved stick. Hurling has similar rules to Gaelic football, although some regard this as having no rules at all. Devotees regard it as an art, maintaining that 'hurling is a game for piano tuners, football is a game for piano removers.'

Opposite: *An old man and* (below) *his donkey.*

To the north of Kilkenny is County Kildare, world famous for its horses. All over its northern region are facilities for hunting, breeding, training and racing horses. Punchestown, near Naas, has been a racecourse since the 19th Century, and the headquarters of Irish racing is at The Curragh, near Kildare Town. This is the largest common in Ireland, and every morning stable lads from the many surrounding stables can be seen putting lithe and graceful horses through their paces. Ireland's major race, the Irish Sweeps Derby, is held at the Curragh every summer. On this day the enclosures are buzzing with activity, the crowd is splashed with colour from women's bright clothes and extravagant hats. The reserved stand becomes a sea of binoculars as the horses approach the winning post. With the sun shining, the breathless pounding of hooves, the powerful movements of glossy-coated horses, and the vivid colours worn by the jockeys crouched low in the saddle provide an unforgettable experience.

Tully, close to Kildare Town, is the home of the Irish National Stud. It began as a stud

Left: *Looking across the lake on the magnificent Powerscourt Estate, County Wicklow with the Sugarloaf Mountain in the distance.*
Below: *The empty shell of Powerscourt House, damaged by fire in 1974.*

farm owned by Colonel William Hall Walker in the early 1900s, who practised his rather eccentric views on breeding horses with considerable success. He believed that the destiny of horses was guided by the stars, and studied the astrological horoscopes of all the foals to decide whether to keep or sell them. In 1915 he presented his stud farm to the British Crown, and it became the British National Stud until 1943, when it was transferred to the Irish government. It has seven handsome stallions with long racing pedigrees, including Tap on Wood, who won the 2000 Guineas and the National Stakes, and Lord Gayle, a fine-looking bay who even at the age of 20 still has a full book of mares.

In most counties in Leinster, there are grand houses dating from the 18th Century, which was a time of great architectural expansion. Not only in Dublin were elegant Georgian houses being constructed, but in the country too. Protestant landowners were very busy building ornate and luxurious mansions to replace cold, uncomfortable medieval castles. Powerscourt, near Enniskerry in County Wicklow, is a fine example. Beautifully laid-out gardens combining trees, flowers, shrubberies, stonework, ironwork, bronze and water are situated in splendour beneath the Sugarloaf Mountain. The present Powerscourt house was designed by Richard Cassels for the Wingfield family and incorporated the original

smaller castle. Its 100 rooms, and a delicate shellwork ceiling, were extensively damaged by fire in 1974. Now it stands open to the skies, the lower rooms full of green plants pressing against the glass windows as though trying to escape. A fireplace balances precariously on top of one high wall, and there is a rather eery atmosphere.

Powerscourt's impressive terraces are paved with black and white mosaic stonework, made from stones collected from the beach at Bray. Two bronze winged horses guard a lake with a high fountain, and there is a wealth of statuary. The man who landscaped these terraces was Daniel Robertson, an eccentric gout-sufferer who apparently directed the work of 100 men with horses and carts while being wheeled around in a barrow clutching a bottle of sherry! The building was finally completed in 1875 and the results are magnificent.

The Great Famine of the mid-19th Century, and the Land Acts at the end of that century, made it too costly for extravagant building, and little of significance was constructed until the last few decades. Nowadays new buildings abound, some more thoughtfully planned than others. After years of economic recession, many of today's relatively affluent generation are rejecting traditional architectural models. Alongside the abandoned and crumbling old stone houses scattered over the countryside are newly built white and brown bungalows, with Spanish arches and ranch-style porches.

Like much of the province, Wexford has assimilated a variety of races, and Wexford Town connects both Norse and Gaelic in its narrow streets and market places. Further north in the heart of the county, is the delightfully situated town of Enniscorthy. The wide River Slaney winds through its steep streets and it is overlooked by Vinegar Hill. County Wexford was the site of much of the fighting in the 1798 Rebellion, and Enniscorthy's streets were twice a savage battlefield. Today when its inhabitants take to the streets, however, it is for the annual Strawberry Fair when countless bowls of local, ripe strawberries are consumed with cream throughout a week of competitions and festivities.

Wexford is reputed to be the sunniest county in Ireland. Many people are attracted to its long beaches, such as the sandy bay at Curracloe, fringed with grassy dunes. The Leinster coast has many deserted beaches that have provided sanctuary for both people and wildlife. The Raven Point Peninsula for example, south of Curracloe, is a three-mile area of forest plantation which has been declared a protected nature reserve.

Leinster is generally more populated and accessible than Munster or Connaught. Its proximity to Dublin and gentler countryside have encouraged modernization. Yet it is a place steeped in ancient ruins and reminders of earlier times, and where traditional ways of life are continued in small villages. Here in the local bar, which may also be the general store, issues of the day are discussed over a glass of stout among hanging rolls of wire, the bacon cutter and shelves containing everything from baked beans to mousetraps. In Ireland, there is always time for the art of conversation.

Above: *A well-kept thatched cottage at Ballaghkeen, County Wexford, nestles into the countryside.*
Below: *This gaily painted former gatehouse to Rathespeck Manor, County Wexford, now provides an eccentric family home.*

Previous pages: *June poppies bring a splash of colour to the ripening wheatfields.*
Opposite: *Many village bars in Ireland, like O'Shea's in Borris, County Carlow, also serve as the general store.*
Overleaf: *An Irish Romany caravan.*

HIS ROYAL TINYNESS

A Terrible ~~...~~ True Story

To Siân, my baby sister S.L-J.

For my mum and her baby brother (Uncle George) D.R.

First published 2017 by Walker Books Ltd
87 Vauxhall Walk, London SE11 5HJ

This edition published 2018

10 9 8 7 6 5 4 3 2 1

Text © 2017 Sally Lloyd-Jones
Illustrations © 2017 David Roberts

The right of Sally Lloyd-Jones and David Roberts to be identified as author
and illustrator respectively of this work has been asserted by them in
accordance with the Copyright, Designs and Patents Act 1988

This book has been set in Avenir

Printed in China

British Library Cataloguing in Publication Data: a catalogue for this book is
available from the British Library

ISBN 978-1-4063-7985-3

www.walker.co.uk

WALKER BOOKS
AND SUBSIDIARIES

LONDON · BOSTON · SYDNEY · AUCKLAND